Extr

Written by: Beau Norton

CEO & Founder of **Health & Happiness Foundation**

Copyright © 2014 - Beau Norton

All rights reserved. No part of this publication may be reproduced, distributed, or transmitted in any form or by any means, including photocopying, recording, or other electronic or mechanical methods, without the prior written permission of the publisher, except in the case of brief quotations embodied in critical reviews and certain other noncommercial uses permitted by copyright law.

My Free Gift to You

5

Introduction: The Importance of Self-Confidence

6

2 Types of Confidence: Ego vs. Body

8

Ego Confidence

10

Body Confidence

18

Integrating Ego and Body Confidence

23

Progress Equals Confidence

25

How to choose the right goal for you.

27

Using Goals Strategically for Increased Confidence

30

Facing Fear - A Step by Step Approach

34

Self-Reliance: The real meaning of Extreme Confidence

41

Additional Habits for Success and Extreme Confidence

46

Success Habit #1 - Daily Reading

47

Success Habit #2 - Daily Journaling and Introspection

49

Success Habit #3 - Healthy Eating and Exercise

51

Everything Is Connected

52

An overview of what we've covered in this book:

53

Conclusion: You Have the Power

56

My Free Gift to You

To help speed up your personal transformation, I have made an affirmation audio track that you can listen to at your convenience. This mp3 uses binaural beat technology, which helps the suggestions penetrate the depths of your subconscious mind where they will begin to shift your beliefs to ones that will better serve you on your journey.

If you are interested, go to the following web address:

www.healthandhappinessfoundation.com/101-affirmations-for-success-audio/

Introduction: The Importance of Self-Confidence

As you probably already know, self-confidence is absolutely necessary if you want to fulfill your potential. If you have anything less than extreme confidence, then you have at least some doubts about yourself and your abilities. It's completely normal to have self-doubt, but I don't want *you* to settle for "normal." Greatness is your aim from now on, and I'm going to give you a formula that you can use to achieve it.

It's been very clear throughout history that the people with high levels of self-confidence tend to go the furthest in their chosen pursuits. People with extreme confidence do not let temporary setbacks slow them down. They have a clear vision of what they want, and they go get it. They almost always get exactly that which they strive for, simply because they feel as if they deserve it and it's already theirs. In essence, confidence can be boiled down to one thing: self-love. You must first feel that you are worthy of what you want. To feel worthy, you must come face to face with your deepest fears and insecurities, because when you finally bring them to the light, they will vanish, bringing you a sense of confidence and peace of mind that you've never felt before. Extreme confidence is possible for you, no matter where you are starting from. Let's find out what it's going to take, shall we?

2 Types of Confidence: Ego vs. Body

On the path to extreme confidence, you will need to work on developing two different types of confidence: *ego* confidence and *body* confidence. These two types of confidence are very different from each other but each compliments the other. You will need to develop both your ego confidence and body confidence in order to reach the highest levels of self-confidence that are possible for you.

Ego confidence is based on your thoughts and the level of belief you have in yourself and your abilities. When you think about doing something and say, "I can do it," and you really believe that you can, then your ego confidence could be considered high for that particular subject. When you strongly believe that you can do something, when you have no doubt in your mind, your ego confidence is high. However, when you are actually performing the task, rather than just thinking about it, is when body confidence comes into play.

Body confidence could also be called "core confidence" or "grounded confidence," because it comes from being rooted in your body rather than in your mind. *Thinking* and *doing* are obviously very different. You may be able to think yourself into believing that you are capable of doing something, but when you actually go to do the thing, it's a whole different story. Let's explore each of these types of confidence a little further.

Ego Confidence

Another term for the ego is "the thinking mind." Basically, your ego is the little voice in your head that talks to you all day long. If you suffer from low self-confidence, this voice is probably very critical and discouraging. Your own inner dialogue has likely been stopping you short of your goals for many years. Perhaps you think you're not good enough, smart enough, skinny enough, outgoing enough, pretty enough, young enough, or old enough to do whatever it is that you really want to do. If you want to be happy, successful, and have extreme confidence, then you have to somehow turn the pessimistic voice in your head into an encouraging one. You must learn to take control of your thoughts and actively change your core beliefs, because your thoughts are the basis for everything that you do in life. You will never take the necessary action unless you first create a more positive attitude for yourself, also known as developing your *ego confidence.*

Developing your ego confidence essentially requires you to *reprogram your mind.* Since every thought you think goes into your subconscious mind and reinforces your core beliefs, it is essential that you find a way to replace the negative voice in your head with a positive one. At first, this will require some effort, but as time goes on, you will begin to develop a positive attitude that serves you everywhere you go.

Fortunately, there are advanced methods that you can use to reprogram your mind very quickly. Thanks to some scientific discoveries, we now have technology that allows you to enter a sort of "hypnotic trance" and implant new thoughts and beliefs into your subconscious mind with minimal effort. By hypnotic trance, I simply mean a very relaxed state of mind that is ideal for learning and mental programming. You don't need a hypnotist or psychotherapist to do this. All you need is a pair of headphones and some audio tracks.

This technology is called *brainwave entrainment*, and it's becoming very popular in the self-help industry. I have used it myself and can attest to it's effectiveness. After 30 days of using the audios and a few other simple techniques, I was feeling more confident and happier than ever. It wasn't fleeting either. I feel the same to this day, actually much better. The techniques I will soon describe to you can be used by themselves without the brainwave entrainment audios, but it will likely take much longer for them to have a noticeable effect. The audios are a great way to speed up your results but are completely optional. You can get the audios at www.bit.do/hypnosismp3. For the purposes of reprogramming your brain for increased confidence, I recommend the *theta meditation* or *delta meditation* audios.

    You will first need to decide what exactly it is that you want. Do you want more confidence in social situations, more confidence in your abilities, or more confidence overall? *Why* do you want more confidence? What will increased confidence bring you? It's important to answer these questions, because your brain will only respond to *specific* messages. Saying "I want more confidence" is not enough. Saying "I want more confidence so that I can make friends easily and enhance my social life" is much better. You could even get much more specific, but having some type of *WHY* is an essential prerequisite.

    Now that you have a compelling reason for increasing your confidence, you will need to write it down in the form of a present tense statement about yourself, often referred to as an *affirmation*. If you want a better social life, you might write something like this: *I am confident and outgoing in social situations, and this allows me to make friends easily everywhere I go.* If you want more confidence to further your career, you might say something like: *My high levels of confidence allow me to easily communicate my ideas to potential employers and business prospects, which leads to an abundance of career and business opportunities for me.* Take some time to write down a minimum of 3 statements that are specific and worded in the present tense as if you had already attained your specific goal. Pretend for a moment that you are already extremely confident, and then write the positive statements from that perspective. This is important.

    Now that you have a clear idea of what you want, you can use the brainwave entrainment audios to bring yourself into a state where your mind can easily accept the statements as true. If you don't have the entrainment audios, you can use any type of relaxing music. Classical music works well. Put some headphones on and listen to the audios for about 5 minutes, or until you feel very relaxed and calm. In this state, the barriers of your conscious mind are brought down and your subconscious mind is susceptible to programming. Under normal circumstances, it may take years of repetition to change the core beliefs that have been holding you back from achieving higher levels of success and confidence, but this method can bring you incredible results in a matter of weeks if you use in consistently. Consistency is the key. Many people use this method and give up far too soon. You must be patient and have faith that these methods will work. 20 minutes per day is really all it takes. If you can dedicate yourself to that, your life will change in ways that completely astonish you. Your dreams are much closer than you might currently believe.

    Once you have let the audios bring your mind and body into a relaxed state, you can begin feeding your mind the positive statements that you have written down. Spend at least 5 minutes on each statement, or focus on one statement for the entire 15 to 20 minute session. Begin the first minute of this exercise by simply repeating the statement to yourself over and over again. Then, for the remainder of the session, repeat the statement once and spend a minute or two visualizing what your life would look like if the statement was indeed true. How would your life be different if you had extreme confidence? What would you do differently? What goals would you strive for if you knew you could not fail? What would your social life be like? Your financial situation? Family life? Imagine your ideal life in as much detail as possible while casually repeating the written statement to yourself every so often. Imagine your success in extreme detail. In it's altered state, your subconscious mind will easily pick up on this message and immediately begin working on bringing that image into your physical reality. This is not magic by any means. It is simply how the human mind works.

      You will become whatever you imagine yourself to be. Many people fail to achieve their dreams and desires simply because they imagine themselves failing! *Worry is the same thing as praying for what you don't want.* Practice thinking about what you *do want*, and you will eventually have it. The way to speed up this process is to use the brainwave entrainment audios.

They will allow you to bypass your self-doubt and criticism and directly influence your subconscious beliefs. Up until this point, no method has been shown to create such dramatic change in such a short amount of time.

Cultivating a strong ego confidence means creating a positive way of thinking. The only way to effectively do so is through repetition. Up until now, you have likely been repeating negative and critical thoughts to yourself over and over again. You must reverse this process by bombarding your mind with positive thoughts on a consistent basis, preferably while in a relaxed state of mind. The process is quite simple, but it will require some initial self-discipline. Commit to performing the previously mentioned mental exercise for a minimum of 15 minutes daily, and you will undoubtedly begin to notice changes in your attitude and behavior.

Ego confidence is only one aspect of extreme confidence. It comes through proper thinking, but as you will soon see, thinking can only take you so far. A foundational, core confidence will take you the rest of the way to the top. It will ensure your success in everything that you do and allow you to overcome obstacles with ease. I refer to it as "body confidence," and it is a necessary ingredient for achieving extremely high levels of self-esteem.

Body Confidence

Body confidence is the type of confidence acquired through action and experience. You can sit at home and work on your mindset, which will help you tremendously, but you will eventually need to take the action required to reach your goals. Only through action can you reach a level of true confidence. You need to gain feedback from your environment in order to learn what it takes to function with maximum effectiveness. This could also be seen as a type of "situational confidence." If you are completely unfamiliar with something, you cannot navigate the situation with extreme confidence. Only when you "learn the ropes" will you be able to navigate through life with ease. As you will learn in this chapter, body confidence is not just about taking action. Anyone can do that. It is more about learning to act while staying calm, centered, and focused.

    We live in a world today that is extremely focused on thinking and "figuring things out." Most people believe that all of their problems can be solved if they can just think up a good enough solution to them. This notion has kept society in a vicious cycle of anxiety, phobias, depression, and just plain old suffering. It's important to realize that your thinking mind, otherwise known as the ego, cannot solve all your problems and actually inhibits your progress in many instances. There is a far greater intelligence in your body, and you may not have even known it was there. This intelligence is sometimes referred to as your "instinct" or "intuition," and you must learn to trust it if you plan on achieving peace of mind and a high level of self-confidence.

Surely, you have had an experience in your life where everything just seemed to go perfectly. You said the right thing at the right time, did exactly what you needed to do, and it all felt effortless. You've likely had this type of experience many times and just weren't aware of it afterwards. When you are talking with a close friend or family member, do you have to *think* about what you are saying? Or does the conversation flow naturally? In situations where you are feeling comfortable and confident, no thinking is required at all. You simply act naturally and *live in the moment* with no stress whatsoever. This would be an example of you displaying high *body confidence*. As you will learn, this state of being is achievable even in situations that would cause the average person massive amounts of stress. Body confidence is *really* what you want. Ego confidence is secondary.

The majority of people are completely out of touch with their bodies and trapped in their heads (thinking too much), so the first step towards cultivating high body confidence is learning how to become grounded within your body. The simplest technique for doing this is to become aware of the sensations in your body parts. Start with your toes. Concentrate on the feeling in your toes for a minute. You should feel a slight tingling sensation. Now, move to your feet, legs, hands, arms, torso, and head. Spend about one minute on each body part until you have become completely aware of your entire body. You should feel very relaxed and energized at the same time when you do this. This is how you get *out of your head* and *into your body*. I suggest you do this exercise for at least 5 minutes daily. Eventually, you will be able to stop your thought process immediately and become completely grounded in your body, which automatically increases your situational awareness and completely eliminates stress and anxiety.

Some people may be very relaxed and grounded in their bodies while at home, but as soon as they are presented with a situation outside of their comfort zone, they become very ungrounded and start thinking in circles. Whenever you experience stress or anxiety, it is always because you have become ungrounded and trapped in the thought processes of your mind. The solution to stress is to learn how to stay grounded in your body under all circumstances. This slows the thinking process and allows you to think and react in a calm and controlled manner, which minimizes your chance of making mistakes or saying something you regret later.

If you lack confidence in yourself, then you are probably fearful of attempting many things, and this limits your opportunities for success in life. The fear you experience is nothing more than a byproduct of your thinking. You experience the sensation of fear in your body. The *thought* causes the *feeling*. You cannot "think away" the feeling of fear. More thinking will only bring you more stress and anxiety. *Less* thinking will bring you peace and calm, but *trying* to think less is futile. The way to *think less* is to *feel more*.

Whenever you find yourself in a situation in which you do not feel confident, remember that the solution to your feelings of doubt is to simply get out of your head and into your body. You can do this easily by attempting to feel the sensations in your body as mentioned above. You can also focus on the inhale and exhale of your breathing, which will also move your awareness into your body. When you do this, you will find yourself acting much more spontaneously. Your words and actions will require no effort. You will be much calmer, and you will be able to think clearly in whatever situation you find yourself in. Always remember, low self-confidence is a product of your habitual ways of thinking, and you can overcome this by consciously shifting your attention to your body.

Integrating Ego and Body Confidence

Ego confidence and body confidence can be worked on interchangeably, and improving one will also improve the other. If the voice in your head is confident, your behavior will reflect that. A calm and confident inner voice will ensure that you *feel* more calm and confident as well. Likewise, when you practice feeling more confident by shifting your attention to your body in stressful situations, your thinking will begin to reflect your feelings. As you gain experience and realize that you can be calm, cool, and collected in any situation, your way of thinking will gradually shift to reflect your behavior.

I encourage you to begin practicing these methods at home. Use the brainwave entrainment audios to reprogram your thinking and practice shifting your attention to your body. Daily practice will ensure rapid results. While I can't promise any results, I can say that these exact methods have helped me go from shyness and insecurity to confidence and peace of mind in a short amount of time. Within a year, I was able to overcome a deep depression and build the confidence required to start my own business. I would not be where I am at today if it wasn't for the strategies I have mentioned and will mention in this book. I hope you consider putting serious effort into practicing what you learn.

Progress Equals Confidence

Thinking good thoughts and feeling good about yourself has a lot to do with the direction in which you perceive your life is headed. If you feel as if you are making no progress towards your goals, then it will be difficult for you to feel happy and confident. Even worse, if you have no goals at all, then it becomes far too easy to view your life as pointless. Getting through each day becomes a chore, and each day tends to feel the same as the last. With nothing to strive for, what's the point of gaining confidence? Achieving greater levels of self-confidence requires you to have a goal and to make steady progress towards that goal.

It's very important that you have at least one clearly defined, long-term goal for yourself. I recommend setting a goal for yourself that is between 6 and 12 months away. This goal will act as motivation for you. With a goal that is within reach, your days will become more exciting and passion-filled. Every step that you take towards your goal will boost your levels of confidence. The more you achieve, the more you will believe in your ability to achieve even greater things. Consistent progress towards a worthwhile goal will ensure that you feel happier and more driven from within each and every day. You may even find yourself jumping out of bed every morning, enthusiastic and excited to start your day. This process of striving for a long-term goal will essentially guarantee a steady increase in your confidence and self-esteem.

There are a few things that you need to know about setting goals. For one, it is absolutely essential that you *write your goals down on paper*. The act of writing your goals down helps to implant them in your subconscious mind, which will help lead you to their achievement. It is also important that you read and review your goals often. This will keep them fresh in your mind and help you to maintain a positive outlook. Lastly, break your bigger goals down into daily, weekly, and monthly goals. This will ensure that you don't get overwhelmed and quit before reaching your goal.

How to choose the right goal for you.

Setting goals is not as simple as it might sound. If you just pick something that sounds nice, then you can't really guarantee your success. However, if you choose your goals wisely, you can guarantee their achievement. Here's how to choose the right goals for you:

First, take a piece of paper and write down a list of 10 things that you would like to have, be, or do in the next year. Take your time to think of 10 compelling things that you desire. Then, go through that list and decide which goals excite you the most when you think about achieving them. On a scale of 1 through 10, write down next to each goal *how strongly you believe* in your ability to achieve that goal. For example, earning a million dollars might be a compelling goal, but if you only currently make $50,000, then a million dollar year is probably not something you strongly believe in. If it is (8, 9, or 10 level of belief), then go for it, but it's important to choose a goal that you truly believe you can achieve. Perhaps increasing your income by 10% is a believable goal for you. Whatever goal you have the highest level of belief in and excites you the most is going to be the goal you achieve the quickest and easiest.

Once you have chosen the most compelling goal for you, write it down on several notecards. Keep one in your wallet or purse, put one by your bed where you will see it every morning, put one on the mirror in the bathroom, put one on the visor in your car, and anywhere else that will force you to be reminded of your goal multiple times every single day. This is important, because the more you are thinking about your goal, the more action you will take to reach it. If you have chosen the right goal for you, however, then you should be thinking about it practically all of the time because it excites you so much. If at any time you find your goal no longer excites you, go back and do the "level of belief" exercise as described above and choose a different goal. It will do you no good whatsoever if you have a goal that does not excite you.

One more thing to note: Having *one* main goal is better than having many. Major goals can always be broken down into many smaller goals, so it is far better to have only one major, long-term goal (6 months - 2 years) for yourself. You must have a chief aim, or else you risk spreading yourself thin. When you have a strong desire for something, you can expect your life to be at least slightly out of balance prior to achieving it. For example, if you want to quadruple your income this year, expect your social life to suffer. By no means is this a bad thing. It simply means you have priorities. Temporary sacrifices are often necessary for great achievements, but you should never feel guilty or ashamed for going after what you want, as long as you are doing so with love in your heart.

Using Goals Strategically for Increased Confidence

Setting goals is essential for all aspects of self-improvement, especially for increasing your confidence. Using specific goal setting strategies can greatly enhance the effect that goal setting has on your levels of self-confidence. This strategy is simple yet profound. Using it will guarantee a steady increase in your confidence over time. Let me explain:

As I mentioned earlier, breaking your long-term goals down into monthly, weekly, and daily goals is very important. This confidence boosting strategy will focus specifically on daily goals, because they are the foundation for all your progress. Small daily accomplishments will accumulate and eventually blossom into something far beyond your current reality. Your future is the result of what you do on a daily basis. This simple goal setting strategy will ensure each day is a success, thus ensuring your future success as well.

Take your chief aim, your long-term goal, and work backwards to plan out the achievement of that goal. If you have set a goal that you hope to achieve in one year, then use a piece of paper to write out what you plan to have accomplished in 6 months, 3 months, 1 month, and 1 week from now. Take your time and use a lot of detail when planning out your goals. This is your life you're planning! Imagine it as you wish it to be.

Once you have done this, you will need to come up with 3 to 5 small tasks that you can do on a daily basis that help move you closer to your goals. Each of these tasks should take no more than 20 or 30 minutes to accomplish. They should be *things that you can do every single day without fail*. This is important, because if you fail to complete these tasks every day, you risk *lowering your confidence* instead of increasing it. For this reason, you should begin with tasks that are quick and easy but enhance your life in some way. To give you an example, here are 3 things that I do daily to improve my life and move me closer to my goals:

- Read for 30 minutes
- Drink 32 ounces of water in the morning before eating
- Review my short and long-term goals

Since these tasks are not difficult for me to do, I do them *every single day without fail*. But that's not quite enough to get the confidence boosting effect. The most important aspect of this is the act of *writing your daily goals down and checking each of them off after completion*. Every time you write a goal down and cross it off your list, your brain releases a small amount of dopamine and other neurotransmitters that make you feel good about yourself. Every goal you cross off your list gives you a small boost in confidence. If you do this consistently, you will actually *become addicted* to the feeling you get when completing your goals. Surely, this is one of the best addictions you could possibly have. You are essentially addicting yourself to success. The more you accomplish, the more driven you become to accomplish even more, and so you get caught in an upward spiral that leads to happiness and great achievement. This growth is exponential. Your small daily accomplishments lead to the accomplishment of your weekly, monthly, yearly, and lifetime goals. Each successful day motivates you to strive for bigger successes. Eventually, you will find yourself accomplishing more in a month than most people accomplish in a year, and with each accomplishment comes greater confidence.

If you are new to the concept of self-improvement and personal evolution, then it is important to start small. Pick 3 simple things that you can do every day without fail. Use a calendar and write down your 3 goals under each day of the month. Every time you complete one, cross it off, preferably with a blue pen (the color blue has been shown to generate more positive emotions). Make sure not to miss a day! If you stick to this strategy, you will notice a dramatic improvement in your levels of confidence and self-esteem within a few short months. You will create the habit of daily progress, and your future will be much brighter because of it.

Facing Fear - A Step by Step Approach

Fear is the one thing that stands between all people and their dreams. Even when everything else is set perfectly in place, fear can easily come in and thwart our desire for improvement, keeping us trapped in a place of perceived powerlessness. In order to ensure that it does not paralyze us completely, we must come up with a strategic, step by step plan for the gradual dissolving of fear. Even before that, however, we must come to see that fear is actually our greatest blessing. Without it, we would never know which direction presents us with the greatest opportunity for personal growth. Almost always, our fear shows us what we have been denying in ourselves. It shows us the face of our own insecurities, not to scare us, but rather to present us with an opportunity to use resistance to our advantage. Moving into the resistance, into the fear, is the only way to evolve into a stronger version of ourselves. Just like a muscle needs the resistance of a heavy weight to grow bigger, we need the resistance of our fear for us to grow into more capable people.

As I mentioned earlier, attempting to "think away your fear" is rarely effective. In most cases, it only causes more anxiety and fear. The only way to truly think away your fear is to start *telling yourself a different story*. You can develop your mindset to the point where fear is diminished, but since fear is a conditioned response experienced *in your body*, the only way to completely overcome fear is to take massive action in the direction of your fear. Only through actual physical experience can you gain the reference experiences required to "change the story" that you tell yourself. The only exception to this is the use of vivid and intense visualization. By imagining experiences in your mind, you can gain reference experiences that translate to your physical reality, but you will find that facing your fears in the physical world is much more life-changing than simply experiencing them in your mind.

Here is a quick example of someone gaining reference experiences to change their underlying core beliefs responsible for their fears and insecurities:

Jane is a shy and timid girl. She gets frightened in social situations and finds it hard to make friends. When Jane was growing up, she would often overhear her parents saying things like "you can't trust anyone these days" or "it's a cold world out there." Growing up with this belief, Jane found it difficult to get close to anyone or put herself out in the open. Unconsciously, she believed that the world was a scary place and people couldn't be trusted. Her reality reflected that belief. But one day, Jane decided that she was sick of living in fear. She decided to change her behavior and face her fears head on. She started going to social gatherings regularly and practiced being vulnerable and open with the people she met. She put herself out there even though it scared her. Not surprisingly, after a few months of behaving in her new manner, her personality began to change. She found herself very relaxed and calm in social situations. She began making friends everywhere she went. How could such a radical change be possible in such a short amount of time? *She changed her story.*

Through experience, Jane changed her beliefs from "you can't trust anyone" to something more along the lines of "people are actually pretty friendly and easy to get along with." Jane needed to get out of her comfort zone and gain real world experience to prove to herself that the world isn't such a cold place after all. You, too, will need to challenge your beliefs if you wish to change. The fact is that most of the beliefs that shape our personalities are based on false information. The people who raised us and the friends we grew up with all played a major role in shaping our beliefs. Well, what if *your* beliefs are nothing more than the *limiting beliefs of others* that have been projected onto you? That is almost always the case. Recognizing this is the first step towards major positive change. You're half way there.

After you have come to terms with the fact that you have some limiting beliefs that are holding you back, you can begin actively challenging those beliefs and "proving yourself wrong." Realize that the reason you haven't been getting everything you want out of life is because of *you*. Even though your beliefs have been shaped by others, they are still *your beliefs*, and that means you are responsible for changing them. I'm now going to provide you with a systematic approach to facing your fears and challenging the belief of "I'm not confident." This method will allow you to gradually realize that you are capable of far more than you once thought possible. As you progress through the levels of this exercise, you will begin to see that what you have been telling yourself is false. You *are* confident.

Keep in mind that this strategy for increasing your confidence is only effective if you follow through with it and *take action*. If you find it difficult to begin, consider using the mental exercises described previously to align your thoughts with what you want to do. In other words, *visualize yourself taking action*. Now, here is what you will need to do:

You will be creating an organized chart for yourself, so take a sheet of paper or use a program like Microsoft Excel to create it. Across the top of the page, write the numbers 1 through 10 with a column under each number (wide enough to write in). The number 1 will represent things that are only slightly outside of your comfort zone. The number 10 will represent things that scare you the most. An example of a level 10 action might be something like speaking in front of a large crowd or going skydiving. An example of a level 1 action might be something like saying hello to a stranger or submitting a job application. Only you know, but these are just some examples to give you an idea of how this works.

The next step will be to fill in at least 3 actions under each number (preferably more for the lower levels of 1 through 5), 1 representing tasks that would be relatively easy for you to do and each subsequent number representing an action of slightly greater difficulty, 10 being your biggest fears. It may take you a while to come up with 3 actions for each level, but it will be well worth your time. This chart will act as your guide on your journey to extreme confidence.

To begin, you will need to *commit to performing one action daily*. Only through consistent action will this strategy be effective. Start with your level 1 tasks and perform one of them daily. You can do a different one every day or the same one, however, you must perform the level one actions *only until they become comfortable*. Once you can accomplish the level 1 tasks with ease, you must move on to the level 2 tasks. The goal is to slowly expand your comfort zone until you are confident and capable of doing much greater things than were previously possible for you. Do the level 2 tasks repeatedly until they become easy for you, then move to level 3 and so on. If you commit to performing one action daily and move up the levels when you feel comfortable doing so, you will see radical changes in yourself within a few months, possibly as little as a few weeks, depending on how quickly you move through the levels. *It does not matter how long it takes*. The important thing is that you are making consistent progress. *You will* make it to extreme confidence if you follow this guide.

Self-Reliance: The real meaning of Extreme Confidence

As you gain new experiences and continue to focus on improving yourself, you will slowly evolve into a greater version of yourself, however, this process never stops. There is no end to your growth. It is important to avoid viewing your efforts as a means to an end, because that will make it very difficult for you to enjoy the process called *life*. Having a destination in mind is very important, but try to see that destination as a stepping stone rather than a final destination.

The good news is that life does get easier as long as you continually force yourself to improve. There will come a time when it will seem as if your efforts have culminated to a final resting place that I like to call *self-reliance*, but it is actually just the place where things become effortless and every moment becomes a joy. This is the state that I have been referring to as *extreme confidence*. It is not a cocky, arrogant way of being, but rather a state of *needing nothing*. This is what we all desire, whether we consciously know it or not.

Self-reliance is something achieved by very few, but it is the mark of true confidence. A self-reliant person does not feel the need to impress others with his or her achievements or knowledge. A self-reliant person feels whole and complete and does things for no other reason than wanting to do them.

Self-reliance could be described as a "lack of ego." This doesn't imply that a self-reliant person is completely enlightened, although they might be, but rather goes to explain that they have reached a point where they are at peace with themselves. This is what most of us *really* want. We may say that we just want more money, a better job, better social skills, or a new car, but what we really want is to feel at peace with ourselves. Striving to accomplish more and more is often times a sign of low self-confidence. We might strive for money and material things because we think it will bring us more recognition and love from others. We don't *really* want the things, we want the peace of mind that comes from feeling as if we are *enough*.

Being a self-help junkie, I completely understand what it's like to want to achieve more and more. It's completely natural to want to be the best we can possibly be. What's important is the underlying *reason* for your efforts. If you want to achieve more so that you can feel more loved, then your efforts will be in vain. You may achieve external success, but you will always feel a lack of worth and the need to accomplish even more if you don't address the reasons for your actions. True confidence will lead to greater success, but only because a confident person is someone who *gives*, not takes. Truly confident people do not need to prove anything. Truly confident people are so full of joy that they can't help but spread those good feelings to others.

    You may perceive certain people as confident, but they may actually be manipulative and egotistical. Some people have mastered *appearing confident*, yet on the inside they suffer from an inferiority complex. Their inner drive comes from a feeling of not being enough and a need to constantly prove themselves. The ones who are truly confident don't need to flaunt it. In fact, the people with true confidence are usually quiet, polite, and do more listening than talking. Confident people feel good about themselves already, so they spend their time *making others feel good*.

I say all this so that you don't get confidence confused with arrogance or achievement. You don't need to achieve anything at all to be confident. You could be poor and on the streets and still have self-confidence. As I said in the beginning of this book, confidence can be boiled down to one thing: *self-love*. If you don't love yourself, no worldly achievement will satisfy you. Striving for more confidence is perfectly fine, as long as you do so for no other reason than to show yourself love and respect.

As you practice the strategies mentioned in this book, you will notice changes in yourself. You will likely go through many phases where you become unsure of yourself and the direction you are headed in. Remember to always stop and ask yourself, "Am I doing this for the right reasons?" If you can confidently say that you are doing what you're doing out of a love for yourself, then you can continue on your path knowing that you are headed in the right direction. If you ever sense that you are doing things in order to *get something* from someone else or to *fill a void* within yourself, then take a step back and simply reevaluate things. No matter what your outwardly goals are, you should always have one underlying reason for your personal growth: *to love yourself more.*

    As you come to love and accept yourself fully, you will lose your need to accomplish things. You will reach the point of self-reliance where you do things simply because you love to do them. Your life will unfold naturally and you will achieve more than you ever thought possible, although those achievements won't mean as much as they once did. You will be happy regardless of what you accomplish. You will not be so inwardly focused on trying to make yourself complete, because you will know that you already are complete and always have been. Although your personal growth will come naturally when you reach a level of self-reliance, it will be for the fulfillment of others and the benefit of humanity as a whole. Your personal journey to extreme confidence is not just your journey to enjoy. Your journey is for the betterment of all. Fill your cup so that it may runneth over and benefit all who surround you. Never forget, *you matter.*

Additional Habits for Success and Extreme Confidence

So far, we've delved into some very transformative techniques and strategies, and I'm confident that you will see great success with them. Now, I'd like to discuss a little more about the *small things* that create self-confidence. After suffering with low self-confidence for years and transforming myself into a confident and successful person, I was able to look back and see exactly what I was doing that allowed me to change. Although I was mostly conscious of these things as I was doing them, it is all much more clear to me now. Who I am today is partly my conscious creation and partly a result of unconscious habits that I created. I offer you the following suggestions so that you can take the mystery out of the equation and direct your life with purposeful intent.

Success Habit #1 - Daily Reading

When I first began taking my personal growth seriously back in 2011, I decided to drastically reduce the amount of time I spent watching television. I would watch football games on Sundays and the occasional basketball game, but that's it. I started valuing my time much more. I felt much better about myself when I spent hours reading a book rather than hours watching television. Today, I only watch television when I'm with my family and they want to watch something. Much of my free time is spent reading. I absolutely love to learn. The habit of daily learning is one thing that I strongly believe is responsible for much of my success and happiness. It gives me the sense that I am continually evolving into a better person, which is extremely satisfying. If you want to increase the quality of your life, then I do believe it is essential that you create the habit of daily reading. I'm not suggesting that you give up all your favorite television shows and replace them with books (that would certainly benefit you though!), but *I am* suggesting that you begin viewing your time as extremely valuable and filling that time with more life-enhancing activities such as reading.

Reading opens up a whole new world of possibilities for you. It exposes you to new information that you can use to improve your life. Reading allows you to form new neural pathways in your brain, which gives you more possibilities for connections between different thoughts. This connection between differing thoughts is also known as *creativity*. Simply reading every day will increase your chances for coming up with brilliant new ideas. It might spark an idea for a new invention, business opportunity, piece of artwork, or simply a solution to a problem you have in your life. It seems so simple, but I strongly believe that reading on a daily basis, no matter the genre, is a very powerful tool for self-improvement. In fact, I have been studying the lives of successful people for over 3 years, and to this day I have not come across a single extremely successful person who does not read books! If that doesn't convince you, I don't know what will.

Success Habit #2 - Daily Journaling and Introspection

If you have an introverted personality like I do, then daily introspection will come natural to you, but I have found journaling to be a powerful tool for manifesting things in your life. For example, I will often read my journal entries from months ago and realize that what I wrote at that time had actually come true for me. This has happened on several occasions. The very act of writing down your thoughts increases the chances that those thoughts will become your reality. I believe this has a lot to do with the power of focused intention. When you are writing, you are usually quite focused on what you are doing, more so than you are throughout the day at least. This level of focus, coupled with a strong desire to achieve greater things, is extremely powerful. For this reason, it is important to only write about things that you want and things that make you feel good. Do not use a journal to gripe and complain about things in your life, because focus on negative things will only attract more negative thoughts to you. Although it might act as a good release of emotions, your best bet would be to either write about positive things or nothing at all.

    If you decide not to start a journal, daily introspection will be of great benefit to you. By that I mean to simply be alone with your thoughts and feelings. Meditation is a great thing, but just sitting alone in silence doing nothing is enough to get the benefits of introspection. By going within yourself and examining your thoughts and feelings, you become more aware of the thoughts that are troubling, and since you increase the awareness of them, you have the opportunity to correct your "flawed" thinking. If you never took the time to examine your own thoughts without judgement, you would make it difficult to improve yourself and your circumstances, because the only way to fix a problem without knowing what's causing it is to stumble upon the solution by accident. Don't rely on accidental improvement. Consciously create your life. It's much more satisfying.

Success Habit #3 - Healthy Eating and Exercise

This one speaks for itself. We all know that a healthy body equals more happiness and higher self-esteem, however, the ways of modern society do make it difficult to make healthy choices. I would estimate that at least 75% of the food you find in a typical grocery store is processed and contains large amounts of added sugar and dangerous chemicals. For that reason, I suggest you shop at places like Whole Foods and get fresh produce from local farmer's markets if possible. Also, juicing fruits and vegetables is very powerful. If you want to lose weight or just feel incredibly energetic and alive, then juicing is a must.

      Exercise is just as critical as healthy eating, not only for the health benefits, but for the rise in self-esteem that comes from looking good. A healthy and fit body equals a healthy and happy mind. Healthy eating and exercise alone can transform your life in many different ways. The difference it makes in the way you feel is well worth the discipline it takes to make it a habit.

Everything Is Connected

When you realize that each area of your life affects each and every other area of your life, you will feel empowered and motivated to take more action. Even the smallest improvement in one area of your life will improve other areas of your life that seem totally unrelated. For example, the food you put in your body affects the chemistry of your brain and makes you feel happier and more energetic. An increase in mood and energy can potentially benefit your social life, because you will act more outgoing and enthusiastic. People will want to be around you more because of your positive energy, which could potentially lead to a career opportunity of some sort, which in turn benefits your financial situation, which in turn makes you even happier and more positive, which leads you to make even better choices, and on and on it goes. One simple decision can change your life forever.

An overview of what we've covered in this book:

- True confidence is a form of extreme self-love, and without that, you will fail to be fulfilled no matter what you do.

- Ego confidence (consciously choosing to believe in yourself) and body confidence (grounded, relaxed, natural state of behaving) can be worked on separately and each will compliment the other, leading to a higher level of overall self-confidence.

- Ego confidence is developed by consciously choosing positive thoughts and repeating them over and over again, preferably while in a very relaxed state. The consistent repetition of statements affects your core beliefs and thus changes your behavior and perspective.

- Body confidence is developed by gaining reference experiences through consistent action and by learning to shift your attention from your mind to your body at any given time. By showing yourself that you can navigate situations in a calm and relaxed manner, you increase the level of belief you have in your abilities and thus dramatically increase both your ego and body confidence.

- Progress equals confidence, so having goals is extremely important. Choose goals that you strongly believe in and that excite you, and you will reach them much quicker. Make small daily progress towards your goal, and you will feel more confident as each day passes. Write your goals down and read them as often as possible in order to maintain a positive outlook for the future and ensure that you continue to stay motivated and take action.

- Facing your fears head on is one of the most effective ways to increase your confidence, because it forces you to "change your story." Facing your fears is not as scary as it might sound if you just use a step by step approach and ease your way into it. Slowly expanding your comfort zone will ensure your success, because you won't feel overwhelmed or overly stressed in the process of taking action. Facing your fears may even become exciting and fun for you using the step by step approach.

- Self-reliance is a state of true confidence, and it is a state of extreme self-love and empowerment. If you want to live an extremely fulfilling life, then your efforts should always be coming from a place of self-love rather than a place of lack or neediness. Strive for self-improvement for no other reason than to give yourself what you deserve. Never manipulate or belittle others in an attempt to increase your own self-esteem. That strategy doesn't work.

- Reading, journaling, and healthy eating are 3 additional things you can do to enhance the confidence-boosting effects of everything else in this book. At the end of the day, it's the small things we do on a daily basis that make the biggest difference in the long run.

Conclusion: You Have the Power

Ultimately, you are the creator of your own reality. Your mind is where it all starts. Your power will come from consciously deciding to think positive thoughts as much as possible. Each positive thought you think will attract more positive thoughts, and those thoughts will inspire you to take positive action that creates wonderful things in your life.

Avoid playing the role of victim, because that is a place of powerlessness. No one else's thoughts, words, or actions can negatively affect you unless you let them. Understand that you are 100% responsible for your thoughts and emotions, and you are therefore responsible for your actions and the circumstances of your life. Taking responsibility is the first step to changing things in your life. Your life won't change unless you change.

You were put on this earth to do great things. I strongly believe that all of us were put here to uplift ourselves and others and experience joy every single day of our lives. I think many of us have gotten distracted by the many perceived problems of the world, and in doing so we have taken our focus away from the positive possibilities. We can't discover solutions by focusing on problems. And so it comes down to one thing: we must choose to direct our energy towards positive outcomes. It's the only way to create positive results.

Thanks so much for taking the time to read this book. I truly hope it helps you achieve the confidence and success that you deserve.

For tons of FREE personal development tools and trainings, or for more about the author, visit www.healthandhappinessfoundation.com

Resources:

Brainwave entrainment audios: http://bit.do/hypnosismp3

Made in the USA
Middletown, DE
30 June 2018